UNDER THE STARS

By Cherie Ralston

KANSAS CITY STAR QUILTS
Continuing the Tradition

ABOUT THE AUTHOR

After growing up in northern Nevada, Cherie now resides in Lawrence, Kansas. She is a self-taught quilter who began quilting 35 years ago. Beginning with traditional piecing, she soon discovered her love of appliqué. With three small children to rear, Cherie found it difficult to find the time to do her appliqué work by hand.

Quilters who were pressed for time turned to the technique of Invisible Machine Appliqué. Cherie experimented with several methods before she perfected her own version that suited her style. Much to the delight of area quilters, she has taught her method of appliqué at several local quilt shops.

Cherie has had her work published in books by Red Wagon, Jan Patek Quilts, Blackbird Designs, Barbara Brackman and Sunflower Pattern Co-Operative. She has had several quilts published in American Patchwork and Quilting.

She has retired from teaching classes for the most part, but continues to teach at Primitives of the Midwest in Lee's Summit, Missouri.

Cherie's favorite quilts combine piecing and appliqué with a star or two or more thrown in for good measure. Her friend Nancy refers to her style as "upscale prim."

This book would not have been possible without the talent and work of the team from *The Kansas City Star.* Doug Weaver always has plenty of encouragement and enthusiasm to share. This year he named Diane McLendon publisher of Kansas City Star Quilts. Her professionalism and spark is a terrific asset.

I've been fortunate to work with my good friend and editor, Edie McGinnis. On a long, laugh-filled ride to and from International Quilt Market in Houston, Texas, she convinced me that I should publish another book. Her editing skills make my instructions clear and concise.

Eric Sears does a remarkable job drawing the diagrams and producing the artwork for the templates. His quick understanding and grasp of what is needed to make the instructions clear is such a valued talent.

Aaron Leimkuhler's photography skills and eye for detail are exhibited in every photograph in this book. Jo Ann Grove's Photoshop skills are invaluable as she tones each picture and gets rid of those dangling threads we may have missed.

I am pleased to have Jane Miller on board as my technical editor. Her remarkable skill at ferreting out mathematical errors gives me confidence that the instructions and templates are accurate.

Amy Robertson is the talented page designer who adds such beauty and warmth to the book.

Lori Kukuk quilted the quilts in this book. She adds texture and enhances the design to the quilts. Lori is truly an artist and I consider her one of the best of friends.

Valuable suggestions and encouragement came from many places. My local quilt shop owners, Sarah Fayman of Sarah's Fabrics and Leslie Ahlert of Stitch-On Needlework were very kind and helpful. Quilters appreciate all the great fabric they make available. My friends Jan Patek, Kathie Holland, Edie McGinnis, Alma Allen and Nancy Moore were always there for me when I had a question, a problem or needed a pep talk.

I have saved the best for last. I want to thank my family. Those near and far, old and new—your support and love make my day. But most importantly, I want to thank my best friend, my husband, John.—*Cherie*

ACKNOWLEDGEMENTS

Under the Stars
By Cherie Ralston

Editor: Edie McGinnis
Designer: Amy Robertson
Photography: Aaron T. Leimkuehler
Illustration: Eric Sears
Technical Editor: Jane Miller
Production Assistance: Jo Ann Groves

Published by:
Kansas City Star Books
1729 Grand Blvd.
Kansas City, Missouri, USA 64108

First edition, first printing
ISBN: 978-1-935362-45-6

Library of Congress Control Number: 2010928976

Printed in the United States of America
by Walsworth Publishing Co., Marceline, MO

To order copies, call StarInfo at (816) 234-4636
and say "Books."

CONTENTS

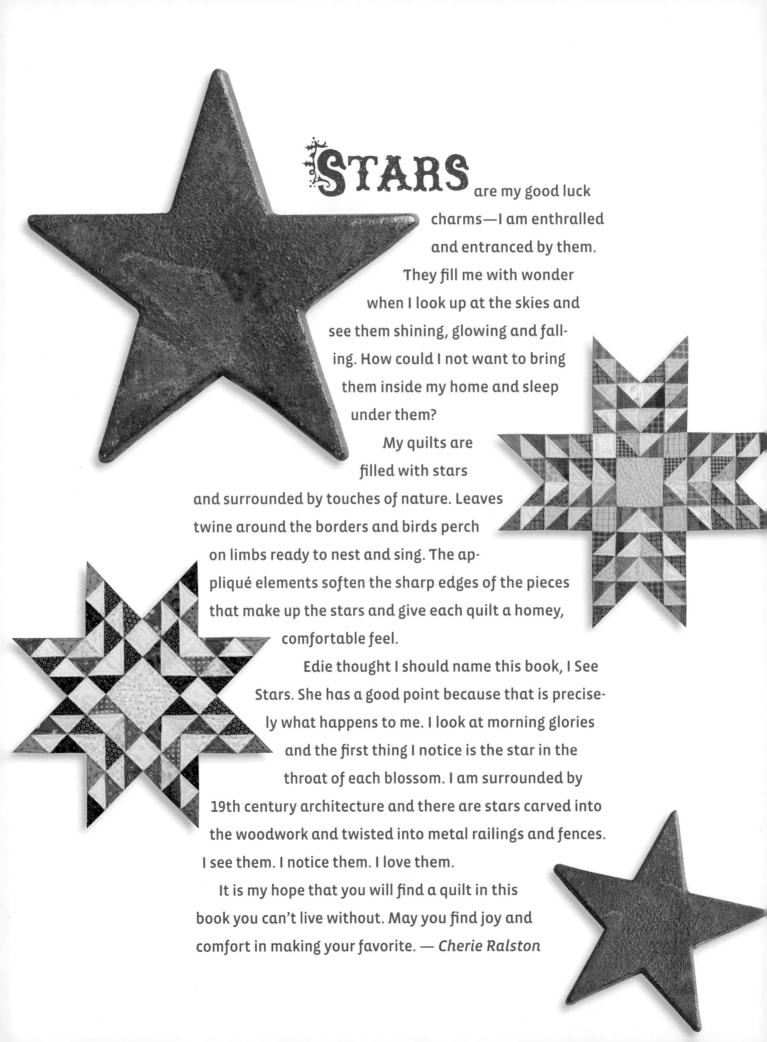

STARS

are my good luck charms—I am enthralled and entranced by them. They fill me with wonder when I look up at the skies and see them shining, glowing and falling. How could I not want to bring them inside my home and sleep under them?

My quilts are filled with stars and surrounded by touches of nature. Leaves twine around the borders and birds perch on limbs ready to nest and sing. The appliqué elements soften the sharp edges of the pieces that make up the stars and give each quilt a homey, comfortable feel.

Edie thought I should name this book, I See Stars. She has a good point because that is precisely what happens to me. I look at morning glories and the first thing I notice is the star in the throat of each blossom. I am surrounded by 19th century architecture and there are stars carved into the woodwork and twisted into metal railings and fences. I see them. I notice them. I love them.

It is my hope that you will find a quilt in this book you can't live without. May you find joy and comfort in making your favorite. — *Cherie Ralston*

Invisible Machine Appliqué

Preparing the freezer paper:
* You need a freezer paper pattern for each piece you appliqué. There are several ways to make the paper pattern pieces.

* **Tracing:** If you want to trace the pattern piece onto the freezer paper, remember to trace onto the shiny side or your pattern will be reversed. Use an indelible pen for tracing.

* **Templates:** If you are making more than one block, you can make plastic templates to use for tracing pattern pieces.

* **Tacking pattern to freezer paper:** You can stack up to 4 sheets of freezer paper, shiny side up. Place the paper pattern on top and tack all the sheets together in several places with the tip of your iron.

* To make berries I recommend quilters buy various hole punches in different sizes from the scrapbooking section of your favorite craft store. The punches make great "berries" out of freezer paper, are easy to remove and you don't have to draw and cut the circles.

Preparing the background fabric
* Cut the background fabric for your blocks 1½" larger than the pattern requires.

* Fold in quarters horizontally and vertically and press lightly.

* Refold in quarters diagonally and press lightly.

Supplies Needed for Invisible Machine Appliqué:
Sewing machine with zigzag capabilities
Open toe sewing machine foot
DMC 50, Mettler 60/2,
   or Aurifil 50 cotton machine embroidery thread
Freezer paper
Water soluble glue stick– such as UHU™
Roxanne's Glue Baste-it™
Paper scissors, fabric scissors
Mechanical pencil
Fine point permanent marker
70/10 denim sewing machine needles
Iron

How To

Preparing the appliqué fabric

✱ Pre-wash all fabric. After you have cut out the paper patterns, iron the shiny side of the freezer paper to the wrong side of the fabric. Leave about ½" between pieces. Cut the pieces, adding about ³⁄₁₆" seam allowance around each shape. If the freezer paper should come loose, just touch it with the iron again. Clip only the inside curves without cutting to the very edge of the paper. Get close though!

Gluing

✱ With the appliqué piece paper side up, run the glue stick on the fabric along the edge of the freezer paper. Glue about 3" at a time. Use the pad of your thumb or finger and start folding the fabric over the edge of the freezer paper. Make the edge as smooth as possible. If you have a severe V-shape, push and roll the area so no raw edges show. You can also modify the severe V-shape by rounding the inside edge for a smoother shape. For a smooth edge, use the tip of a seam ripper, stiletto or mechanical pencil to position the fabric while it is still wet with glue. If your fingers get sticky, use a wet paper towel to clean up.

✱ If the appliqué piece has a point (such as with a leaf, star etc.) fold the tip in first followed by the sides. You don't have to turn under seam allowances that will be over-lapped by other appliqué pieces.

Machine set up:

✱ Use the same thread (DMC embroidery thread 50, Aurifil 50, or Mettler machine embroidery thread 60) in the bobbin as on top of the machine. If you have a machine that has a bobbin case with a finger that can be threaded (Bernina), thread this also. This keeps the thread pulled to the back of your work.

✱ Your thread should always match the appliqué pieces; not the background fabric.

✱ Adjust your machine for a short, narrow zigzag. Always practice on a scrap of fabric before stitching your block.

Stitching

✱ With Roxanne's Glue Baste-it™, glue the appliqué pieces to the background. Begin stitching, sewing right next to the edge of the appliqué piece. One stitch should go into the background, the next one should just barely bite the appliqué piece. Stitches should less than ⅛" apart. Overlap a few stitches at the beginning and the end.

✱ If you have a flower that is layered, stitch those layers together first and cut the paper and extra layers from the back before stitching it to the background.

To remove the paper:

✱ After all of the pieces have been stitched down, turn the block over to trim away the background fabric under the appliqué. Trim so you have ¼" seam allowance. Or you can make a slit large enough to pull the paper out.

✱ Submerge the appliquéd block in lukewarm water for 30 to 60 seconds. Squeeze out the excess water. Gently pull the block on the diagonal to release the paper. Quickly pull out the paper. Rinse the block in clean water and wrap it in a towel to remove the excess water. Toss your block in the dryer with a couple of dry towels to dry the block as quickly as possible and prevent any colors from bleeding. Press with a steam iron from the back.

Half-Square Triangle Units

I like to use the following methods when I make half-square triangles.

1. The Angler 2™ Pam Bono Designs, Inc. I use this tool if I am making many half-square triangle units—especially if I'm working on a scrappy quilt where I want to use many different fabrics. This method uses squares to make 2 half-square triangles at once. The Angler 2 is a thin plastic sewing guide you tape to the bed of your sewing machine. It's marked with diagonal lines and ¼" seam allowance lines that are used as a guide when sewing. Carefully follow the directions given in the package and you'll be ready to do some speedy piecing.

✱ You need to know a little math when you use this tool, **very little**!

✱ Add ⅞" to the finished size of the half-square triangle you are making. That's it!

✱ Most of the half-square triangle units in this book are 2" finished with the exception of the outer border on Bye, Bye Birdie which are 4" finished.

✱ To make the 2" half-square triangle units, simply cut 2⅞" squares, one light and one dark. Place a light square atop a dark square with right sides facing. Line up the top point of the squares under your ¼" sewing machine foot. Line the bottom point up with middle line on the Angler2. Sew, keeping the points matched up with the line until you have finished the seam. Flip it around and repeat for the other seam. Cut apart the units and press toward the darker fabric.

2. Thangles™, or Triangles on a Roll™ are 2 other tools I use when making a lot of half-square triangle units. Purchase the appropriate size paper. Place a light fabric atop a dark fabric with right sides facing, pin the paper in place and sew on the lines indicated. Cut apart, press the seam allowance toward the darker fabric. Tear the paper off.

3. Grid Method. This method is done by drawing a grid on a light fabric paired with a dark. Add ⅞" to the finished size of the desired half-square triangle. Draw diagonal lines to use as a sewing guide, and then stitch ¼" on either side of the diagonal lines. Cut apart on the solid lines and press the seam allowance toward the darker fabric.

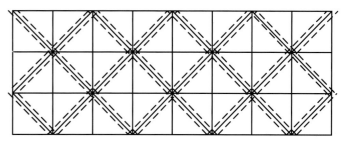

QUILTS & PROJECTS

SOLITUDE

Quilt size: 86" x 86" • Block size 20" x 20"

Cutting Instructions for Blocks

✳ From the cream fabrics, cut
  ✳ 144 – 2⅞" squares (for half–square triangles)
  ✳ 9 – 4½" squares
  ✳ 36 – 2½" squares
  ✳ 36 – 6½" corner squares
  ✳ 9 – 9¼" squares cut from corner to corner twice
    on the diagonal.

✳ From the blue fabrics, cut
  ✳ 144 – 2⅞" squares (for half–square triangles)
  ✳ 72 – 2⅞" squares. Cut each square from corner to corner
    once on the diagonal to make 144 triangles

Fabric Requirements:

1/2 yard each of 9 different cream fabrics

1/3 yard each of 9 different blues (medium to dark)

3 1/2 yards of a large print blue for the setting
  squares and triangles

To Make Half–Square Triangles

✳ Draw a line from corner to corner on the reverse side of
  the 2⅞" cream squares. Place a cream square atop a blue
  square and sew ¼" on either side of the drawn line. Cut
  along the drawn line, open and press with the seam going
  toward the darker color. If you would rather use another
  method, refer to the options on page 9 or
  use your favorite method.

✳ Make 288 blue and cream half–square
  triangles.

Block construction
Make the following components.

✷ Make 72 of Unit A.

✷ Make 36 of Unit B.

✷ Make 18 of Unit C.

✷ Make 18 of Unit D.

✷ Once you have all of the cutting done and these units made, the block will go together very quickly.

✷ Assemble the center of the star using units C and D and the 4½" cream squares you cut previously. Press and set aside. Make 9.

 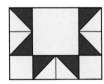

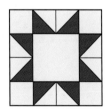

✷ Using 2 of the Unit A components, one Unit B component and the cream triangles you cut previously, assemble these sections as shown. Make 36.

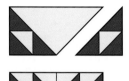 

✷ Add the 6½" corner squares as necessary and assemble 9 blocks. See the illustration below.

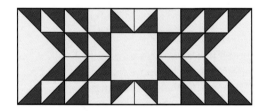

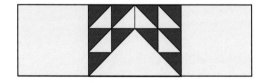

*To make the setting squares and triangles, cut the follow-
  ing pieces from the 3½ yards of large blue print:
    *4 – 20½" setting squares
    *2 – 30" squares. Cut each square from corner to corner
      twice on the diagonal to make 8 side-setting triangles.

*2 – 15¼" squares. Cut each square from corner to corner
  once on the diagonal to make 4 corner triangles.

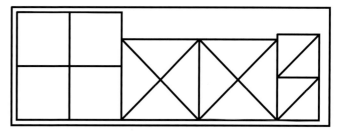

*Assemble the quilt as shown below.

Bye, Bye Birdie

Quilt size: 84" x 84"

Cutting Instructions

✴ From the beige fabric, cut the center square 25"–26". Trim to 24½" after the appliqué work is finished.

✴ Cut out the tree, limbs, bird, 3 stars and leaves. You will find the templates on pages 62–66.

✴ You will need to cut the following leaves:
  ✴ Leaf 1 – cut 8
  ✴ Leaf 2 – cut 10 and 5r
  ✴ Leaf 3 – cut 6 and 6r
  ✴ Leaf 4 – cut 6 and 7r

✴ Appliqué in place using your favorite method. Trim the block to 24½".

First border

✴ From the beige fabric, cut 4 – 7¼" squares. Cut the squares from corner to corner twice on the diagonal.

✴ From ¼ yard of green/brown, cut 5 – 7¼" squares. Cut the squares from corner to corner twice on the diagonal.

✴ Assemble 4 strips as follows:

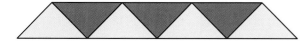

✴ Sew 4 corner units.

Fabric and Notions Requirements:

1 yard beige for center, first border triangles and large sawtooth border
1/3 yard brown for tree trunk and limbs
1/3 yard 2 different greens for leaves
1/4 yard green/brown for first border
3/4 yard 1 red for second border, sawtooth stars, and leaves
3/4 yard additional red for bias vine and leaves
1/3 yard additional red for leaves
1 fat quarter each of 6 additional reds for sawtooth stars and leaves
1/3 yard each of 9 different golds
1/3 yard each of 9 different beiges
1 1/4 yards gold for setting triangles around the sawtooth stars
2 1/3 yard medium beige for appliqué border background and final border
6" square light blue for appliqué stars
1 fat quarter dark blue plaid for baskets
#18 – 3/4" Clover Bias Tape Maker
See templates on pages 62-66.

Bye, Bye Birdie

* Sew the strips to the sides and the top and bottom of the center square. Add the corner units.

Second border

* Cut 2 – 2½" x 30½" red strips and sew to the sides.

* Cut 2 – 2½" x 34½" red strips and sew to the top and bottom.

Third border

* Follow the directions below to make 16 sawtooth stars using the beige, red and gold fabrics.

For each block

* From beige background, cut:
  * A – 4 – 2½" squares
  * C – 1 – 5¼" square

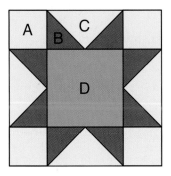

* From gold fabric cut:
  * D – 1 – 4½" center square

* From red fabric cut:
  * B – 4 – 2⅞" squares. Draw a diagonal line from corner to corner on the reverse side of the squares.

Sewing

* Place 2 of the red squares on opposite corners of the background square. Sew ¼" on each side of the drawn lines. Cut apart on the drawn line. Press open.

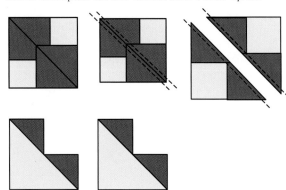

✱ Place a red square on the corner of the large triangle, right sides together, making sure the drawn diagonal line runs from the corner to the center. Sew ¼" on each side of the drawn line. Do this on both pieces. Cut apart on the drawn line. Press open.

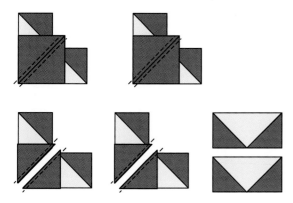

✱ Assemble the block as shown. Make 16 blocks.

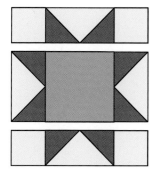

✱ Cut the setting triangles for the sawtooth star border. From the 1¼ yard of gold fabric, cut 6 – 12⅝" squares (a). Cut each square from corner to corner twice on the diagonal.

✱ Cut 8 – 6⅝" squares for corner setting triangles. Cut each square from corner to corner once on the diagonal.

✱ Make 2 of each of the following strips.

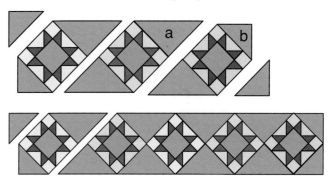

✱ Attach the side borders first, then the top and bottom.

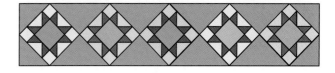

✱ The quilt is now 57" unfinished after the sawtooth star border has been attached.

BYE, BYE BIRDIE

Fourth border appliqué baskets and vines

✳ From the medium beige fabric, cut
   ✳ 2 side borders 10¼" x 57"
   ✳ 1 top and 1 bottom border 10¼" x 76½"

✳ From the fat quarter of dark blue plaid, cut 4 baskets. You will find the template on page 64.

✳ From ¾ yard red, cut 1½" bias strips. Pull the strips through a #18 Clover bias tape maker. You will need approximately 9 yards of bias vine.

✳ You will need to cut the following leaves from the red fabric. You will find the templates on page 64.
   ✳ Leaf 5 – 40 and 40r
   ✳ Leaf 6 – 12 and 12r
   ✳ Leaf 7 – 14 and 14r

✳ Refer to the photo and pin or baste the appliqué pieces in place in a whimsical fashion. Appliqué the leaves, vines and baskets using your favorite method.

✳ Attach the side borders first, then the top and bottom borders.

Final border 4" finished sawtooth

✶ Using the remaining beige and gold fabrics from
  the sawtooth star blocks, cut 40 beige and 40 gold
  4⅞" squares. On the light square, draw a line diagonally
  from corner to corner. Place a light square atop a dark
  square with right sides facing. Sew a ¼" seam allowance
  on each side of the drawn line. Cut apart on the drawn
  line. Press the unit open with the seam toward the darker
  fabric. Refer to page 9 for other methods of making
  half-square triangles.

✶ Sew 20 sawtooth units together. Make 4 strips.

✱ Attach the first strip to the bottom, sewing to the point shown in the drawing. Then attach the right side, the top and finally the left side. Go back and finish sewing the bottom strip in place.

Sew to here

SPRING PLEASURES

Quilt size: 86" x 86" • Block size: 20" finished

Cutting Instructions

* From the beige background fabrics, cut 9 – 20½" squares. For placement purposes, fold each square in quarters, press lightly. Fold in half again on the diagonal and press again.

* For each block, cut out the following appliqué pieces. You will find them on pages 67–70.
  * 1 – A – red
  * 1 – B – black
  * 1 – C – brown
  * 4 – D – green
  * 4 – E – red
  * 4 – F – bright gold
  * 8 – G – green
  * 8 – H – green
  * 4 – J – dark gold

* Refer to the drawing on page 27 and place the appliqué pieces on the block. Baste in place then appliqué using your favorite method. Make 9 blocks. Set aside.

To Make the Sashing

* From the black fabrics, cut 24 – 2" x 20½" strips
* From the red fabrics, cut 16 – 2" squares.

Fabric Requirements:

1 yard each of 5 different beige backgrounds
1 fat quarter each of 6 different reds
1/2 yard each of 5 different greens
2 1/4 yards of another green for borders
1 fat quarter each of 5 different bright golds
1 fat quarter each of 7 different dark golds
1/2 yard each of 7 different blacks for circles, sashing, border stems and leaves
1 – 9" square each of 3 different browns for small stars

See templates on pages 67–70.

✱ Assemble the blocks and sashing as shown below. Set aside.

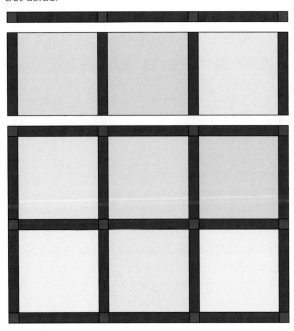

✱ From the 2¼ yards of green fabric, cut 4 borders 10½" x 76½" lengthwise. **Baste** the borders to the quilt center in the order given in the diagram below.

✱ Once you have all 4 borders **basted** to the quilt center, go back and baste the top right side closed. At this point, all the borders will be attached. Now you are ready to place the appliqué pieces.

✱ From the black fabric, cut out the following appliqué elements. You will find the templates on pages 67–70.
   ✱ 16 stems
   ✱ 4 corner stems
   ✱ 92 – Leaf G
   ✱ 40 – Leaf H
   ✱ 47 – Leaf K

✱ Prepare the stems and leaves for appliqué.

✱ Refer to the diagram on page 27 and place the appliqué elements on the 4 borders. Pin or glue in place. Pin the corners carefully. You won't be able to do the appliqué work on them until you have re-attached the borders.

✱ Take the borders off. Stitch all the appliqué elements in place except those that go on the corners.

✱ Reattach the borders permanently as shown in the drawing. Appliqué the corner stems and leaves in place.

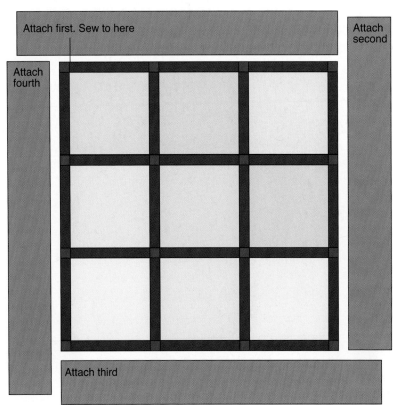

Autumn Stars

Quilt size: 88" x 88"

Cutting Instructions
✶ From the beige fabric, cut
　✶ 216 – 2⅞" squares

✶ From the pumpkin fabric, cut
　✶ 216 – 2⅞" squares

✶ Make 432 half–square triangles.

To Make Half-Square Triangles
✶ Draw a line from corner to corner on the reverse side of the 2⅞" beige squares. Place a beige square atop a pumpkin square and sew ¼" on either side of the drawn line. Cut along the drawn line, open and press with the seam going toward the darker color. If you would rather use another method, refer to the options on page 9 or use your favorite method.

✶ From the pumpkin fabrics, cut
　✶ 40 – 2⅞" squares. Cut each square from corner to corner once on the diagonal.
　✶ 16 – 2½" squares
　✶ 4 – 4½" squares

✶ From the beige fabric, cut
　✶ 32 – 2⅞" squares. Cut each square from corner to corner once on the diagonal.
　✶ 20 – 2½" squares
　✶ 5 – 4½" squares

✶ From the eggplant fabric, cut
　✶ 4 – 8½" squares
　✶ 4 – 16½" squares
　✶ 8 – 8½" x 16½" rectangles
　✶ 12 – 6¼" squares
　✶ 3 – 9¼" squares. Cut each square from corner to corner twice on the diagonal.

Fabric Requirements:
1/3 yard each of 9 different pumpkin fabrics
1/3 yard each of 9 different beige fabrics
6 yards eggplant fabric
1/2 yard each of 2 different green fabrics
1/3 yard of another green fabric
#18 3/4" Clover bias tape maker

See templates on page 71.

★ Refer to the diagrams below to assemble the following units.

Unit A
Make 5

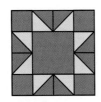

Unit B
Make 4

Unit C
Make 8

Unit D
Make 20

Unit E
Make 4

Unit F
Make 16

Unit G
Make 12

★ Use one Unit C and one Unit D to make 8 components like the diagram below.

★ Use one Unit E and one Unit F to make 4 components as shown.

★ Use one Unit C, one Unit G and one Unit F to make 12 components like the diagram below.

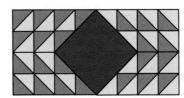

✱ Assemble the quilt in strips as shown below using the 3 components you have just made along with Units A and B.

✱ Sew the strips together as shown below.

Make 2

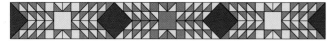

Make 2

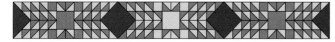

Make 1

Make 2

Appliqué border

✱ Cut 4 strips 8½" x 80½". Set aside.

✱ Prepare the leaves, berries, stars and vines for applique using your favorite method. You will find the templates on page 71.

✱ From the two ½ yard cuts of greens, cut approximately 9 yards of 1½" bias vine. Sew the strips together to form one long strip and press the seams in one direction. Pull the strip through a Clover #18 bias tape maker. Refer to the instructions included in the Clover package if necessary.

✱ From the green fabrics, cut out the leaves using the templates on page 71. You'll need 100 leaves so cut 20 using each template.

✱ Cut 49 large berries, 30 small berries and 3 stars from the leftover pumpkin fabric. You will find the templates on page 71.

✱ The borders are all similar, yet different. The layout isn't exactly the same for all 4 borders although the same number of leaves (25) is used on each. The berry placement is also whimsical, as are the stars. Refer to the photo and place the the vines, leaves, berries and stars to suit yourself. Appliqué in place using your favorite method.

✱ Attach the borders as follows:
  ✱ Attach the top border. Sew only to where indicated. Next sew the right border on, then the bottom and the left border. Go back and sew the top left hand side of the top border closed.

Sew
to here

Stark Raven Mad

Quilt size: 48" Square • Block size: 12" Finished

Sun Blocks

✳ Make 5 and set aside.

✳ Use the freezer paper piecing method for piecing the sun blocks.

✳ Copy the freezer paper templates found on pages 75–76 for the sun blocks. You'll need to make one copy per block.

✳ Stack 4 sheets of freezer paper—approximately 8" x 11"—for each sun block, shiny side up. Place 1 photocopy of the pattern on top of this stack.

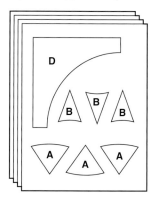

✳ Press the tip of your hot iron to all the x's marked on the pattern. You may have to hold it in place for 1–3 seconds.

✳ Use a cutting mat, an Exacto knife and ruler to **accurately** cut all of the pieces apart on the drawn straight lines. Use scissors on those that are curved. Be sure to transfer the placement lines onto the paper side of the freezer paper D templates.

✳ Carefully pull the freezer paper apart.

✳ Cut one freezer paper center circle C. Transfer the placement lines onto the paper side of the freezer paper.

Fabric Requirements:
1 yard beige for appliqué background, sawteeth and star
1 fat quarter green for leaves
1 fat eighth black for ravens
1 fat eighth brown for stems
1/3 yard gold for suns
1/3 yard beige for suns
1 yard blue for suns, star background and sawteeth
5/8 yard large red print

Supplies:
Freezer paper

See templates on pages 72–76.

Preparing the fabric

⁕ Iron the shiny side of the freezer paper patterns to the wrong side of the appropriate fabrics, leaving about ½" between each piece. Using your rotary cutter and mat, cut out each piece adding ¼" seam allowance on all sides. The Add-a-Quarter ruler works great for the straight edges— the ledge on the ruler fits right up against the paper and makes it easy to add an accurate seam allowance. If you wish, you may use a regular quilting ruler to add the ¼" seam allowance Use scissors for the curved pieces.

⁕ Use a pencil or fabric pen to draw the seam line onto the reverse side of the fabric on the inner and outer curves. Transfer the placement lines onto the seam allowance of the sun center and the 4 blue background pieces.

Sewing the units:

⁕ Pin piece A to piece B. Match the points and line up the edges of the fabric. This will automatically line up the paper edges. Stitch along the edge of the paper.

⁕ Leave the paper in place on both A and B pieces. Do this for all 12 units. Press all of the seams in the same direction, toward the darker fabric.

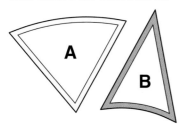

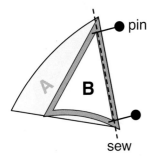

pin

sew

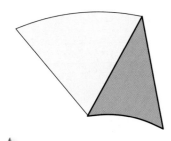

⁕ Pin the units into pairs and sew the next seam. Leave all of the freezer paper attached. This prevents the fabric from stretching. If it comes loose, press again.

⁕ Continue stitching until you have a ring. Once the ring is pressed, remove the paper.

⁕ Match the placement lines on the center circle to the inside points of the ring. Pin well. Sew the center in place.

⁕ Sew the 4 corner units (D) into one unit as shown.

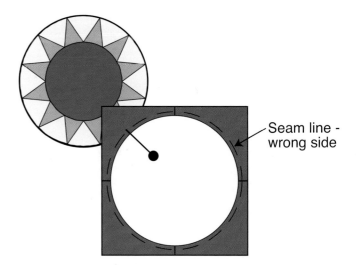

Seam line - wrong side

⁕ To set the sun into the D unit, place the pieced sun on the table right side up. Place the D unit on top of the sun as shown. With right sides together, pin one of the points of the pieced sun to one of the placement lines on the D unit.

⁕ Move to the next sun point and D unit placement line. Continue until you have gone all the way around the sun.

⁕ Now begin lining up the drawn seam lines that you made earlier of the A piece and D piece. Place 2–3 pins between the pins that you have already placed at the points. Continue all the way around.

⁕ Sew on the drawn line, making sure to remove the pins as you come to them. Press carefully, making sure you don't distort the block.

Raven blocks

* For each raven block locate the templates on pages 72–73 and cut the following:
    * 1 – 12½" square from beige background
    * 1 black raven
    * 1 stem
    * 7 green leaves and 3 reverse green leaves
      —or any combination you chose.

* You may notice all 4 blocks are different. Refer to the photo for placement.

* Appliqué the pieces in place and set aside.

Star block

* For the star block, cut
    * 1 beige star—you will find the template on page 74
    * 1 – 8½" square from blue background

* Appliqué the star in place and set aside.

Sawtooth border

* From the blue fabric, cut
    * 46 – 2⅞" squares

* From the beige fabric, cut
    * 46 – 2⅞" squares

* Make 92 blue and beige half-square triangles.

To Make Half-Square Triangles

* Draw a line from corner to corner on the reverse side of the 2⅞" beige squares. Place a beige square atop a blue square and sew ¼" on either side of the drawn line. Cut along the drawn line, open and press with the seam going toward the darker color. If you would rather use another method, refer to the options on page 9 or use your favorite method.

* Sew 23 half-square triangles together as shown below. Make 4.

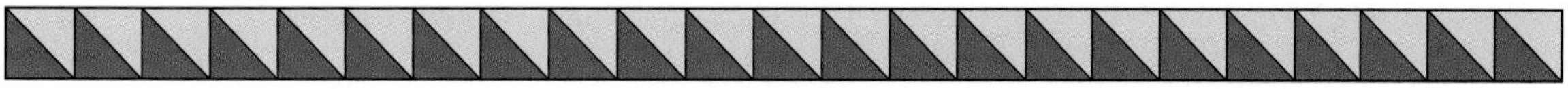

Red border

* From the red fabric, cut
  * 2 – 8½" x 36½" strips

* Once you have made all of the blocks and borders, assemble the quilt as follows:
  * Stitch the 5 sun blocks and 4 raven blocks together as shown in the diagram below to form the center of the quilt. Sew one red border strip to the bottom.

* Sew the star block to the bottom of the red side border strip. Attach this strip to the quilt body.

* Attach the right sawtooth strip as shown on the drawing, stopping about 3" from the end. Attach the bottom strip, then add the left side strip. Sew the top sawtooth strip on last. Once those are sewn, go back to the first sawtooth strip and close the last 3".

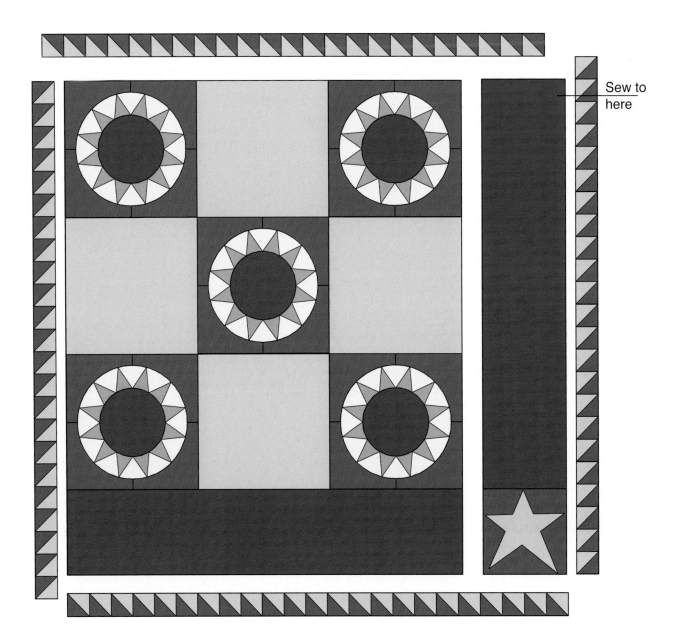

Sew to here

38

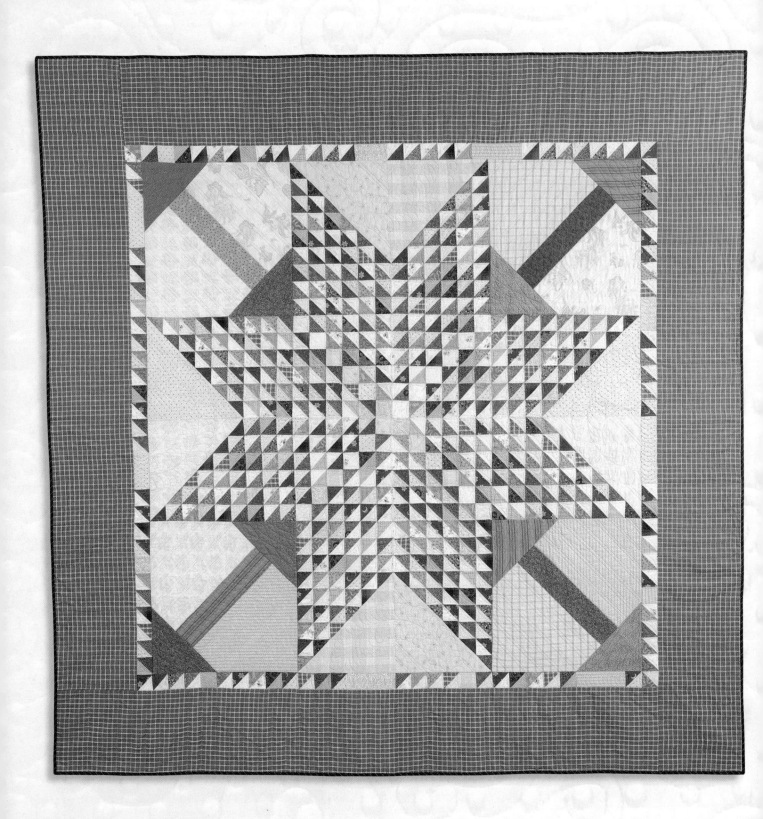

PINE TREE

Quilt size: 84" x 84" • Block size: 30"

Cutting Instructions

✳ From the beige fabrics, cut
  ✳ 240 – 2⅞" squares (Use these for half–square triangles)
  ✳ B – 24 – 2½" squares
  ✳ C – 4 – 12⅞" squares cut from corner to corner once on the diagonal
  ✳ D – 8 pieces (Follow Diagrams 1 through 3 on page 42 to make the templates for this piece)

✳ Green:
  ✳ 240 – 2⅞" squares (Use these for half–square triangles)
  ✳ A – 12 – 2⅞" squares cut in half diagonally
  ✳ E – 4 – 8⅞" squares cut in half diagonally
  ✳ F – 4 pieces (Follow Diagrams 1 through 3 on page 42 to make the templates for this piece)

✳ You will need 480 – 2" finished green/beige half-square triangles—384 for the blocks and 96 for the sawtooth border.

To Make Half-Square Triangles

✳ Draw a line from corner to corner on the reverse side of the 2⅞" beige squares. Place a beige square atop a green square and sew ¼" on either side of the drawn line. Cut along the drawn line, open and press with the seam going toward the darker color. If you would rather use another method, refer to the options on page 9 or use your favorite method.

Fabric and Notions Requirements:

4 1/2 yards assorted greens
  (this includes 2 1/4 yards for the border)
3 1/2 yards assorted beiges
Freezer paper

✳ For the D/E/F trunk unit cut an 18" x 18" square of freezer paper. Make 2" and 8" marks as shown in Fig. 1.

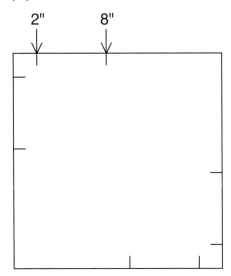

Fig. 1

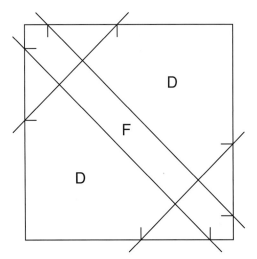

Fig. 2

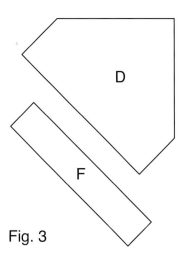

Fig. 3

✳ Draw diagonal lines as shown in Fig. 2.

✳ Using your rotary cutter or scissors, cut on the drawn diagonal line. Fig. 3. These are now your templates. Iron the freezer paper templates onto the corresponding fabrics (green trunk, beige background). Using your ruler and rotary cutter, cut out 4 trunks and 8 backgrounds, making sure you add ¼" seam allowance all the way around.

Block construction
✳ Assemble the 4 blocks as follows:

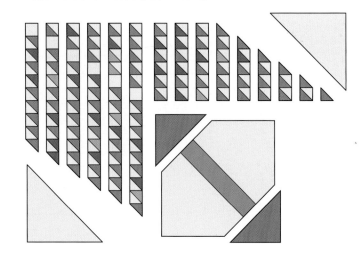

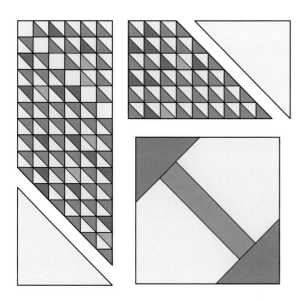

★Sew the 4 blocks together as shown below.

43

PINE TREE

Sawtooth border

✷ For the sawtooth border, you will need the remaining 96 half–square triangle units you made earlier. You will also need to cut the following pieces from the beige fabrics:
  ✱ 6 – 2½" squares
  ✱ 3 – 2½" x 4½" rectangles
  ✱ 4 – 2½" x 6½" rectangles
  ✱ 1 – 2½" x 8½" rectangle

✷ Refer to the drawing on page 45 and assemble the sawtooth borders. Attach the sawtooth borders by sewing the sides on first, then the top and bottom.

Final border

✷ Cut 4 – 10½" x 74½" strips. Attach the first border sewing to the place indicated in the drawing on page 45. Attach the second, third and fourth borders. Go back to the place you stopped sewing on the first border and sew the last of the seam closed.

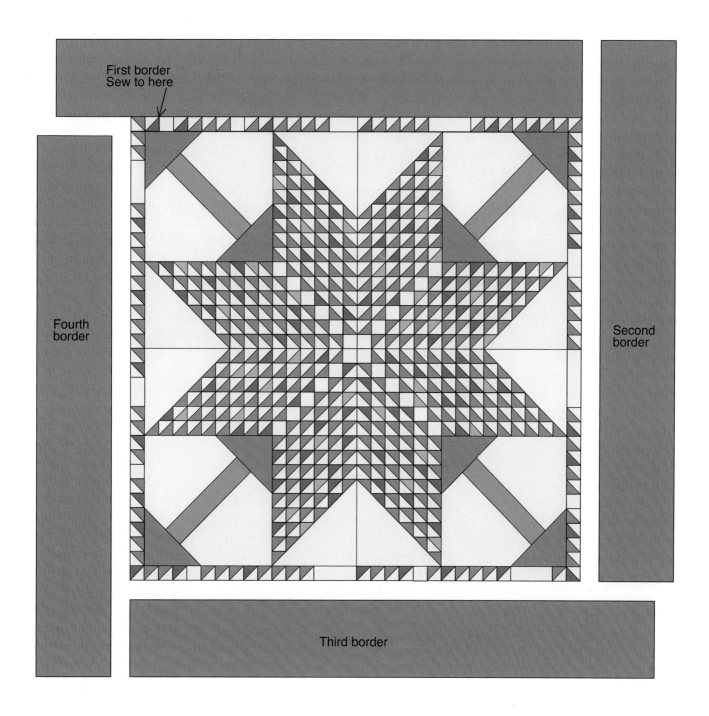

First border
Sew to here

Fourth border

Second border

Third border

Quilt size: 44" x 44"

Cutting Instructions
* From the red fabrics, cut
    * 80 – 2⅞" squares (Use these to make half–square triangles.)
    * 16 – 2½" squares
    * 16 – 2⅞" squares cut from corner to corner once on the diagonal

* From the beige fabric, cut
    * 80 – 2⅞" squares (Use these to make half-square triangles.)

* From the gold background fabric, cut
    * 4 – 12½" squares
    * 4 – 8⅞" squares cut from corner to corner once on the diagonal

* Make 160 half-square triangles for the star.

To Make Half-Square Triangles
* Draw a line from corner to corner on the reverse side of the 2⅞" beige squares. Place a beige square atop a red square and sew ¼" on either side of the drawn line. Cut along the drawn line, open and press with the seam going toward the darker color. If you would rather use another method, refer to the options on page 9 or use your favorite method.

Fabric Requirements:
1 1/4 yards total of a variety of red fabrics
7/8 yard total of a variety of beige fabrics
1 yard gold background

✱ Piece the star together as shown in the diagrams below.

 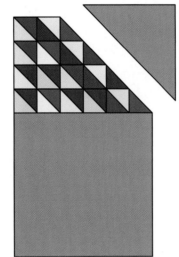

Make 4

✱ Sew the four sections together before adding the sawtooth border.

Sawtooth border

✱ You will need 62 beige and red half-square triangles for the sawtooth border. See the instructions on page 47 for making half-square triangles if necessary.

✱ From the red fabrics, cut
  ✱ 31 – 2⅞" squares (Use these squares to make half-square triangles.)

✱ From the beige fabrics, cut
  ✱ 31 – 2⅞" square (Use these squares to make half-square triangles.)

✱ From the gold fabric, cut
  ✱ 10 – 2½" squares,
  ✱ 3 – 2½" x 4½" rectangles
  ✱ 2 – 2½" x 6½" rectangles.

✱ Assemble the strips as shown in the drawing on page 49. Attach the side borders first, then the top and bottom.

Pocket Calendar

Directions
✱ Cut the linen 7⅛" x 15". Zigzag around all 4 sides.

✱ Fold each end under ¼" and top stitch.

✱ Fold in half and press.

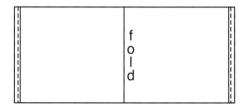

✱ Place the linen wrong side up.

✱ Fold both ends toward the center until the linen measures 8" across. Press.

✱ Measure over to the right of the fold 2" and up from the bottom 1½". Begin cross stitching at this point.

✱ Follow the chart and cross stitch using one strand of floss over 2 threads.

Supplies:
32 count gold linen 8" x 16"

DMC floss
  3051 – green
  435 – gold
  919 – rust
  3047 – cream

Crescent Colours Hand Dyed Floss
  Tartan Plaid – blue

Pocket calendar
  3 3/4" x 6 3/8" (available at office supply stores)

See cross stitch charts on pages 53 and 77.

Cover assembly

✳ Place the linen right side up on your ironing board.

✳ From the center fold, measure 3⅞" to the right and the left. Place a pin at each point. This will be the edge of the book cover.

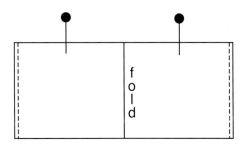

✳ Fold the sides inward toward the center fold, stopping at the pins.

✳ Pin in place—top and bottom.

✳ Sew a scant ¼" seam all the way across the top and the bottom.

✳ Turn right side out, taking care to make the corners and edges neat. Press.

✳ Slip your calendar inside.

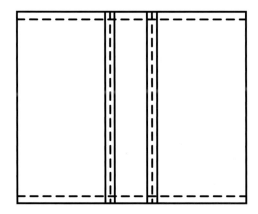

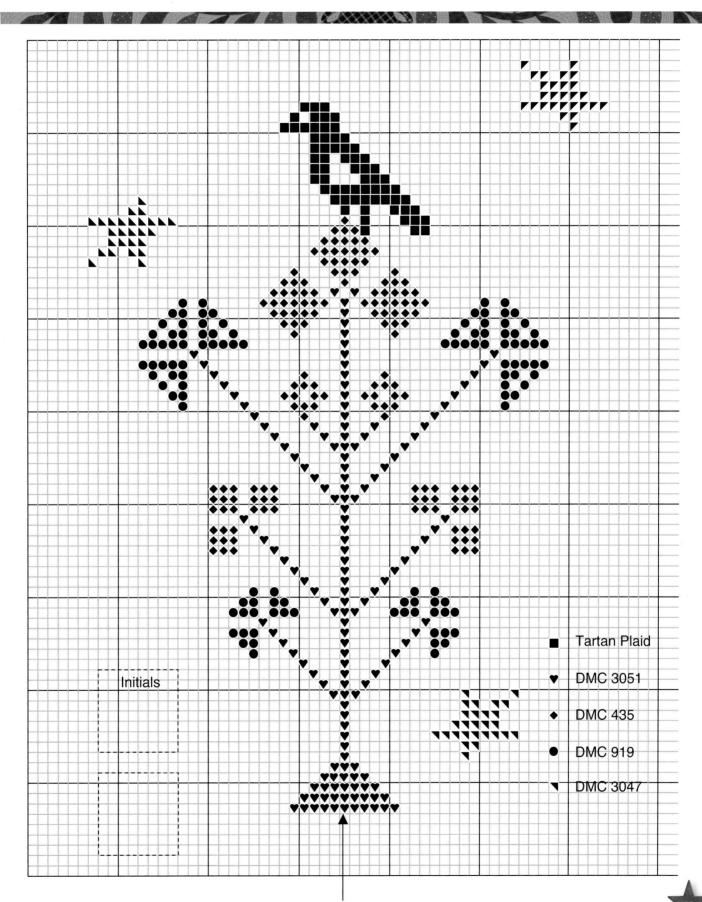

Initials

■	Tartan Plaid
♥	DMC 3051
◆	DMC 435
●	DMC 919
◤	DMC 3047

Note: Use the chart on page 77 for the initials.   Start here

ABCDEFGHIJKLMN
OPQRSTUVWXYZ

QUAKER PINCUSHION

Project size: 15" x 3½"

Directions

✱ Follow the chart and cross stitch using one thread of floss over 2 threads.

✱ Once the stitching is done, press with the stitched side down. Measure ¾" away from the stitching on the reverse side of the fabric. Mark, with a pencil, all the way around the stitching so you can see your sewing line.

✱ Fold the homespun fabric in half lengthwise. Press. Place the cross stitch on top of the homespun right side down. Pin to prevent shifting.

Pencil line/stitching line

ИML\KIIHGⱯƎⱭƆᗺⱯ

ƵYXWVUTꙄЯQꟼO

Opening

✱ Sew along the pencil line leaving an opening at one of the small ends. Turn right side out leaving the 2 layers of homespun together. Make sure the corners are nice and neat.

✱ Now separate the 2 pieces of homespun and fill with the crushed walnut shells. Whip stitch closed.

✱ Use a couching stitch and matching thread to attach the chenille yarn. Follow the seam line where the cross stitch linen meets the homespun.

A B C D E F G H I J K L M N
O P Q R S T U V W X Y Z

Fabric and Notions Requirements:

32 count linen – 6" x 17"
Crescent Colours Hand Dyed Floss – Tartan Plaid and Ruby Slippers
Blue homespun – 12" x 17"
Crushed walnut shells (available at pet stores and packaged as Lizard Litter)
1 yard cotton chenille yarn

See cross stitch chart on pages 77 and 78.

Black box

✴ Paint the outside of the box and lid using the Teddy Bear Tan paint. Let dry.

✴ Measure down 1" from the top edge of the box and place a strip of painter's tape all the way around. Paint the top edge Licorice. Remove the tape.

✴ Paint the lid Licorice over the Teddy Bear Tan.

✴ Trace the star stencil onto the Mylar or freezer paper. Use the Exacto knife to cut out the stencil. Tape it in place on the lid. Using Teddy Bear Tan and the stencil brush, stencil the star using a pouncing motion. Repeat the process for the circle. Stencil the circle in the center of the star.

✴ Trace the leaf stencil. Be sure to include the dotted lines that will help you line up the stencil for continuing around the box. Cut out the stencil. Tape the strip in place on the box. With the Licorice, stencil. Move the stencil, lining up the dotted lines. Continue around the box.

✴ Let dry, then sand lightly to give the box an antique look. Wax with Briwax. Let dry, then buff with a clean soft cloth or 0000 steel wool.

Red box

✴ To make the red box, paint the outside of the box and the lid Light Red Oxide.

✴ Measure 1" down from the top edge of the box and place a strip of painter's tape all the way around. Paint the top edge Teddy Bear Tan. Remove the tape.

✴ Stencil the star, leaf motif and circle inside the star Teddy Bear Tan. Refer to the directions given for the black box if necessary.

✴ Let dry, then sand lightly to give the box an antique look. Wax with Briwax. Let dry, then buff with a clean soft cloth or 0000 steel wool.

Supplies:
8" papier mâché box (4" tall)
1" foam brush
Stencil brush
Mylar or freezer paper
Exacto knife
1/2" blue painters tape
Briwax – light tan

Folk Art™ paint for black box
    Teddy Bear Tan
    Licorice

Folk Art™ paint for red box
    Teddy Bear Tan
    Light Red Oxide

See stencil patterns on page 79.

HEART SACHET

Project size: 3" x 5½"

Instructions

✶ Trace the heart pattern onto freezer paper and cut out.

✶ Layer 2 pieces of fabric together with right sides facing.

✶ Iron the heart pattern onto the fabric. Sew along the edge of the freezer paper.

✶ Cut the heart out leaving ¼" seam allowance all the way around.

✶ Clip the inner curve and turn right side out.

✶ Fill with lavender (or fill with stuffing if you would rather have a pincushion).

✶ Whip stitch the opening closed.

Fabric and Notions Requirements:
2 – 4" x 6" scraps of brown velveteen
   or fabric of your choice
1/2 cup dried lavender

See template on page 80.

TEMPLATES

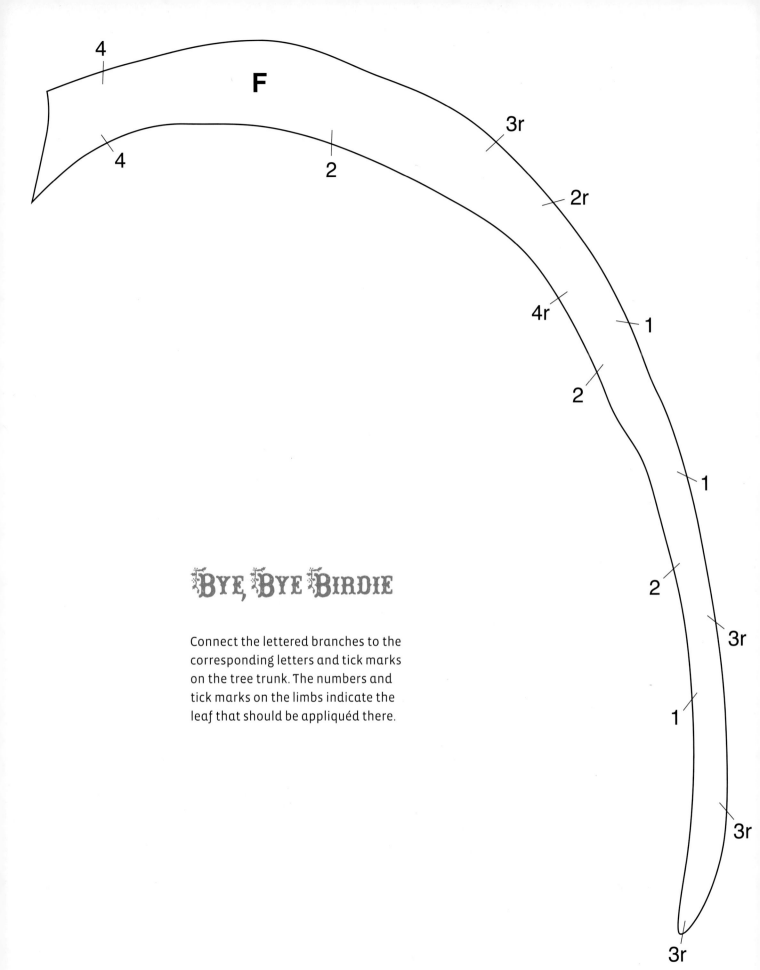

F

4

4

3r

2

2r

4r

1

2

1

2

3r

1

3r

3r

Bye, Bye Birdie

Connect the lettered branches to the corresponding letters and tick marks on the tree trunk. The numbers and tick marks on the limbs indicate the leaf that should be appliquéd there.

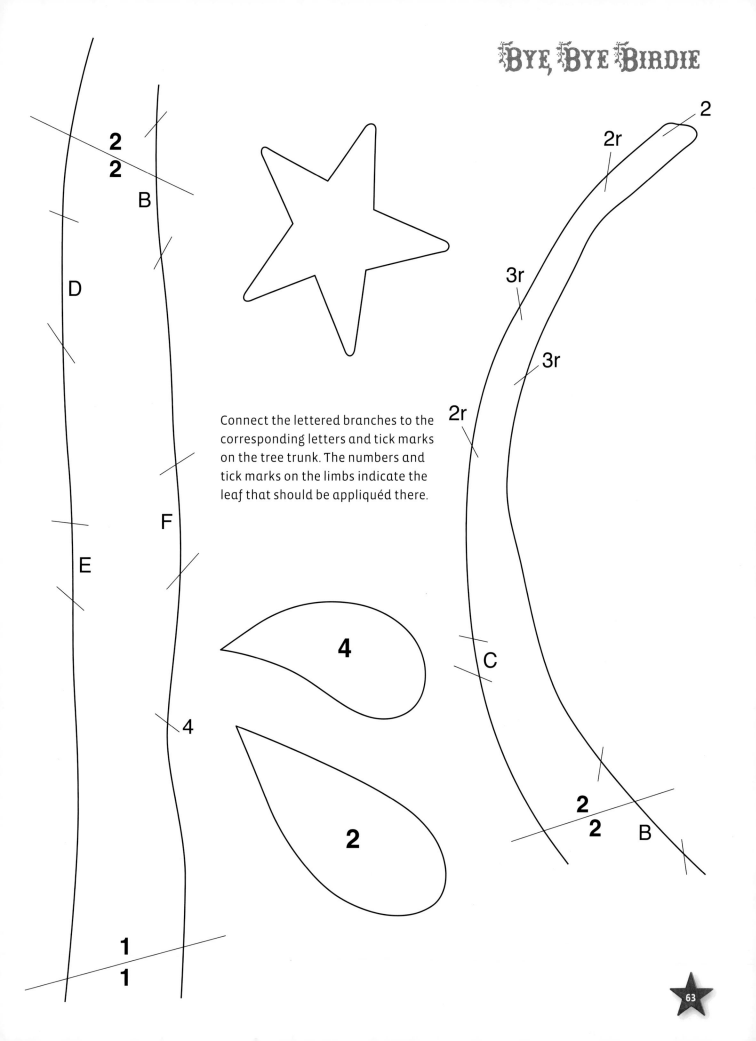

Connect the lettered branches to the corresponding letters and tick marks on the tree trunk. The numbers and tick marks on the limbs indicate the leaf that should be appliquéd there.

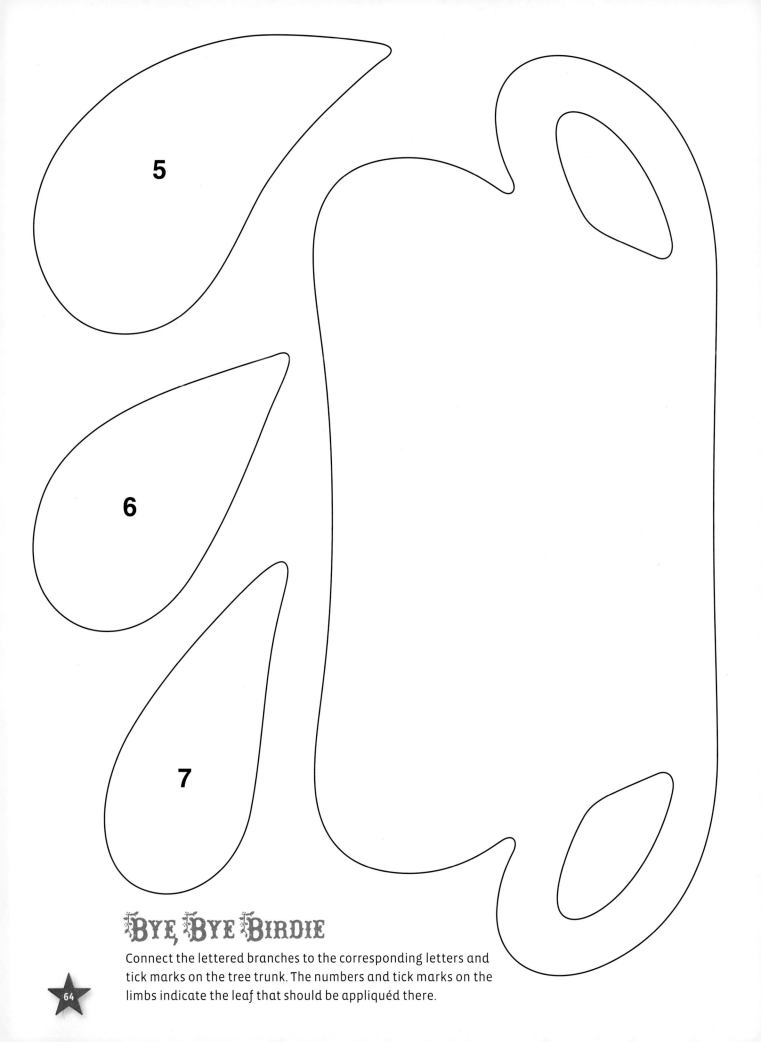

BYE, BYE BIRDIE

Connect the lettered branches to the corresponding letters and tick marks on the tree trunk. The numbers and tick marks on the limbs indicate the leaf that should be appliquéd there.

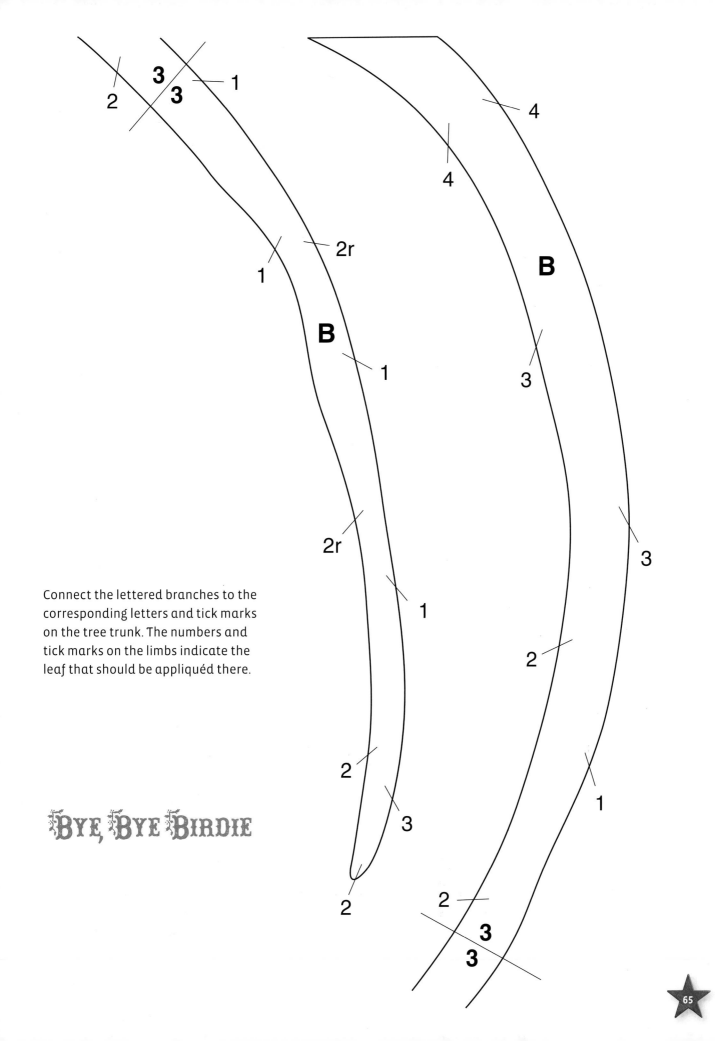

Connect the lettered branches to the corresponding letters and tick marks on the tree trunk. The numbers and tick marks on the limbs indicate the leaf that should be appliquéd there.

BYE, BYE BIRDIE

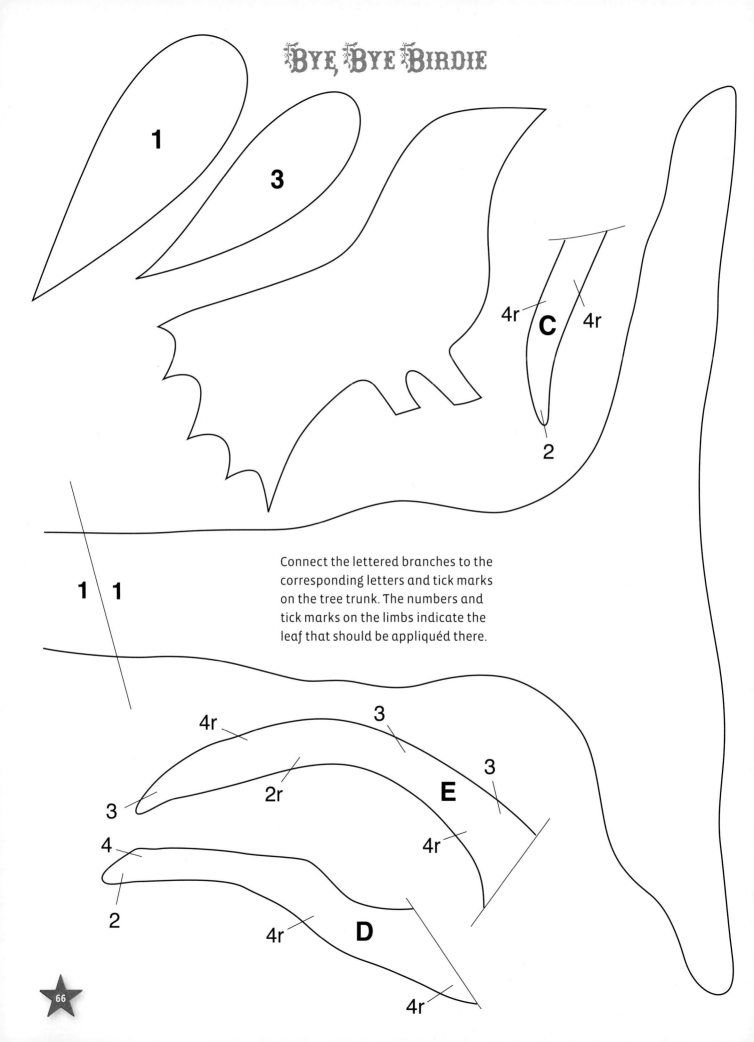

BYE, BYE BIRDIE

1

3

4r **C** 4r

2

1 | **1**

Connect the lettered branches to the corresponding letters and tick marks on the tree trunk. The numbers and tick marks on the limbs indicate the leaf that should be appliquéd there.

4r

3

3

2r

3

3

E

4r

4

2

4r **D**

4r

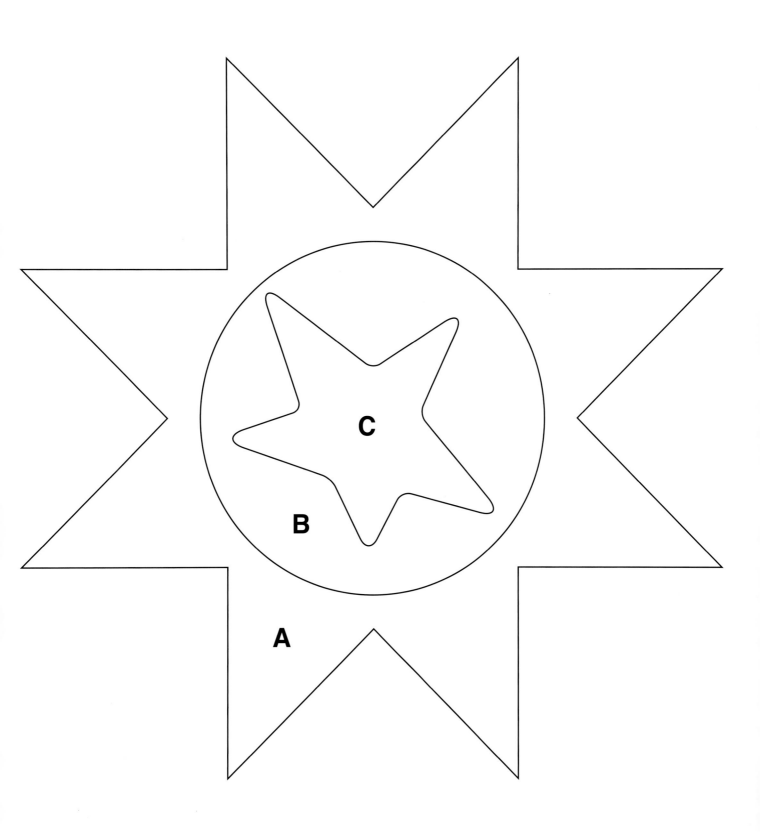

A

B

C

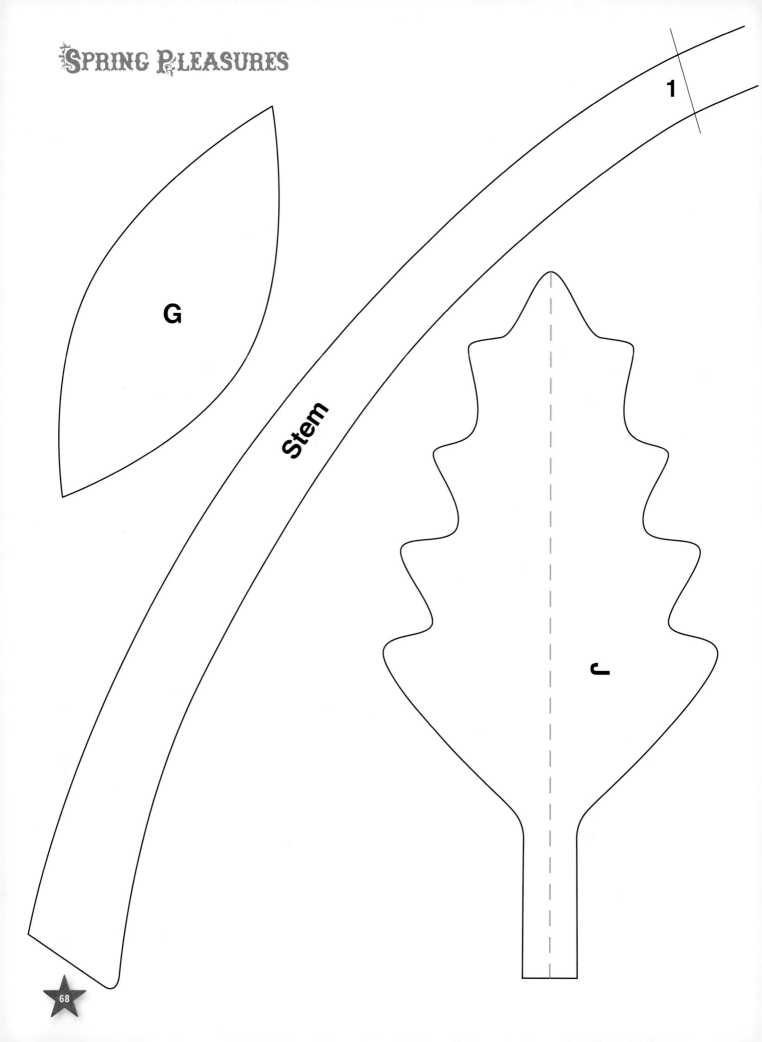

SPRING PLEASURES

G

Stem

1

J

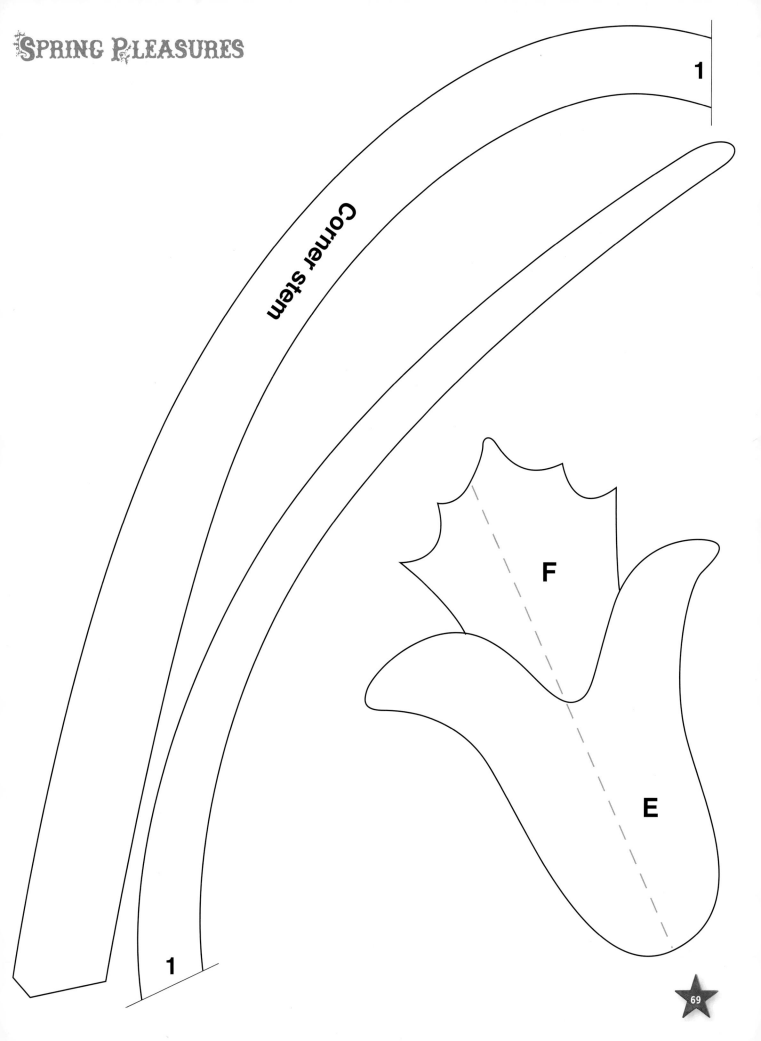

Spring Pleasures

1

Corner stem

1

F

E

69

D

H

K

1

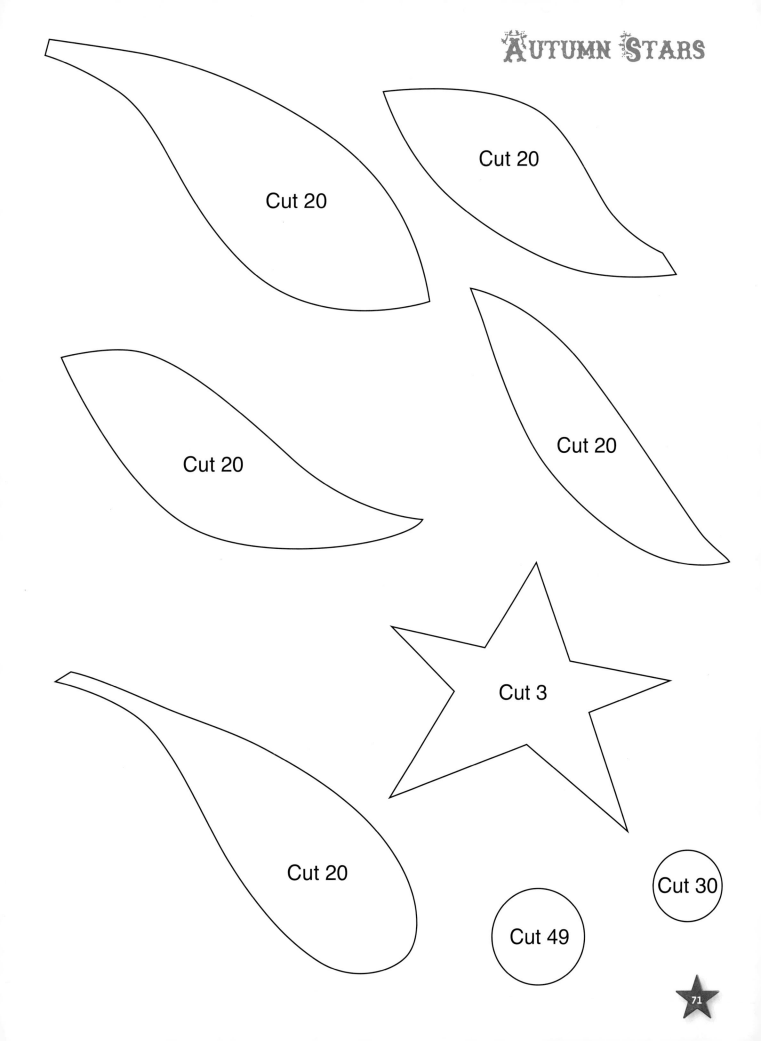

Cut 20

Cut 20

Cut 20

Cut 20

Cut 20

Cut 3

Cut 49

Cut 30

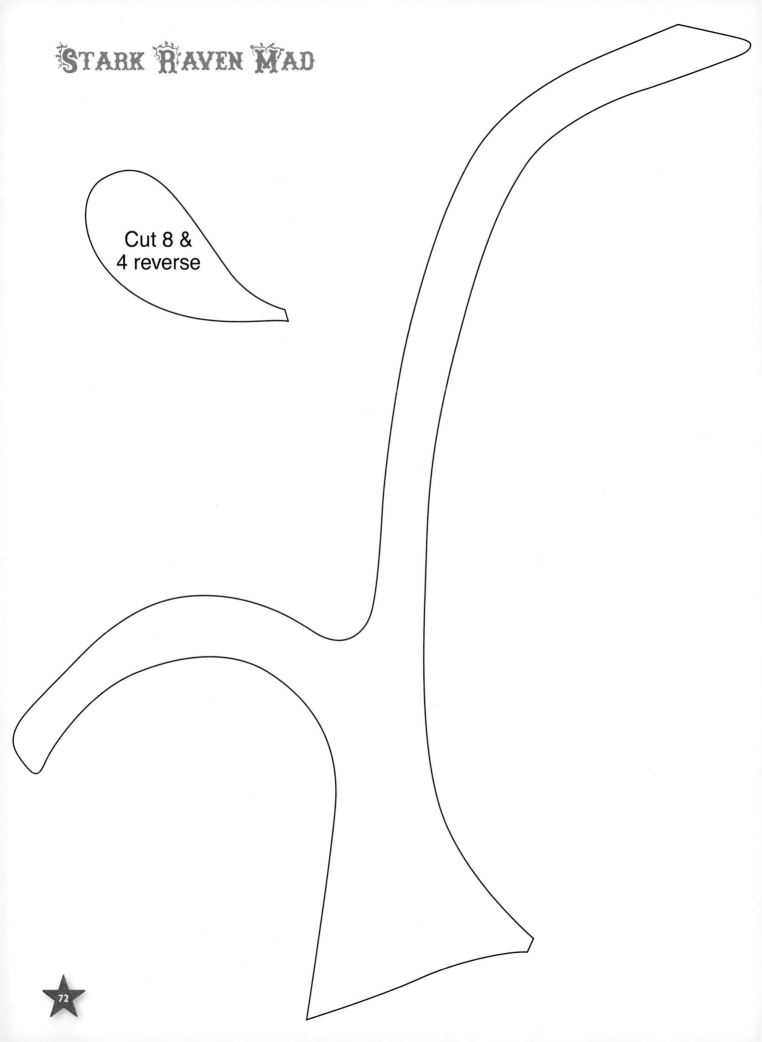

STARK RAVEN MAD

Cut 8 &
4 reverse

72

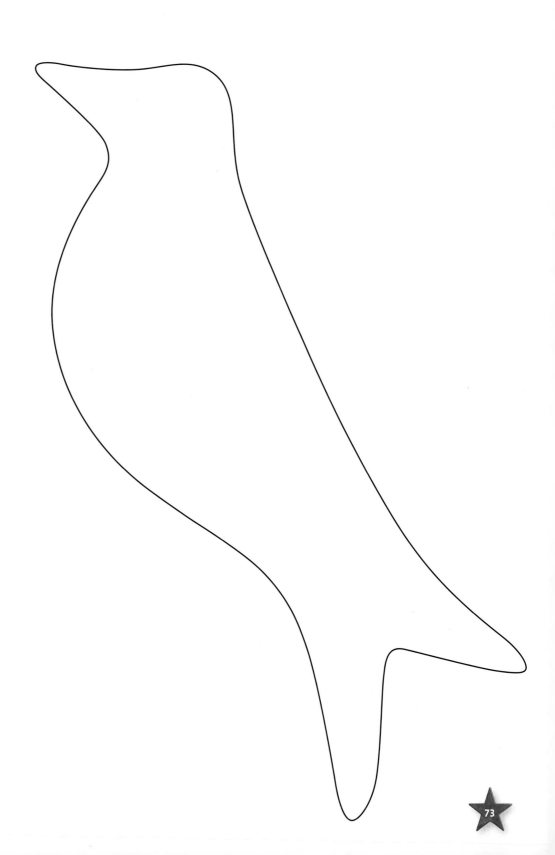

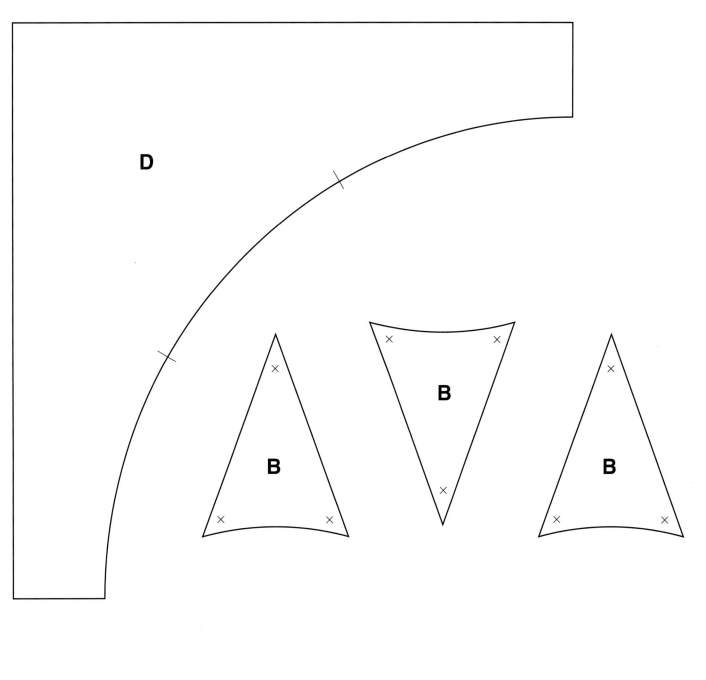

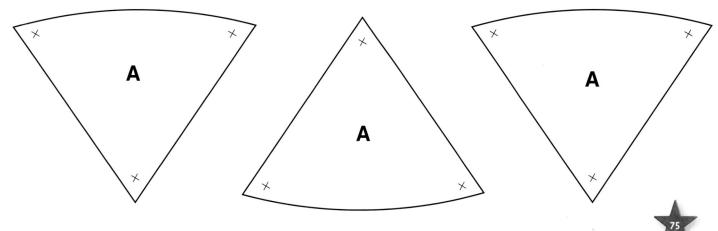

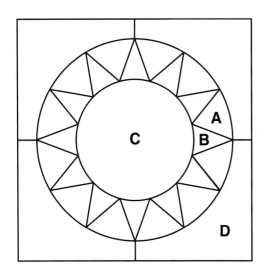

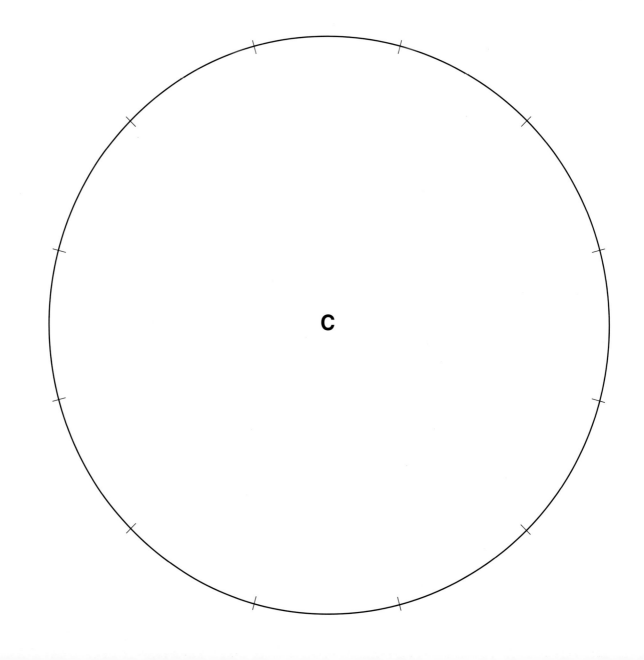

C

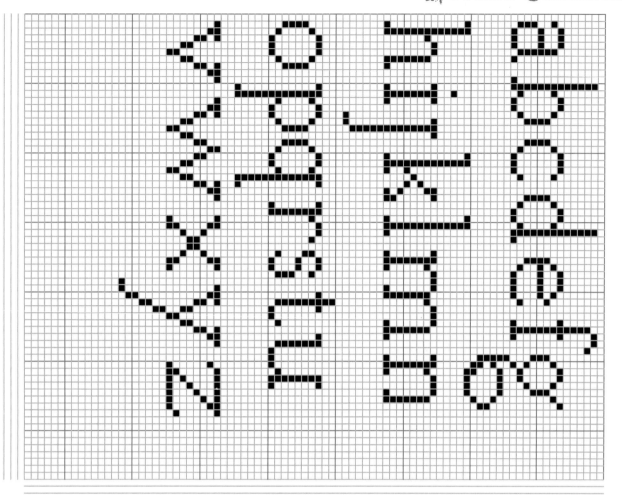

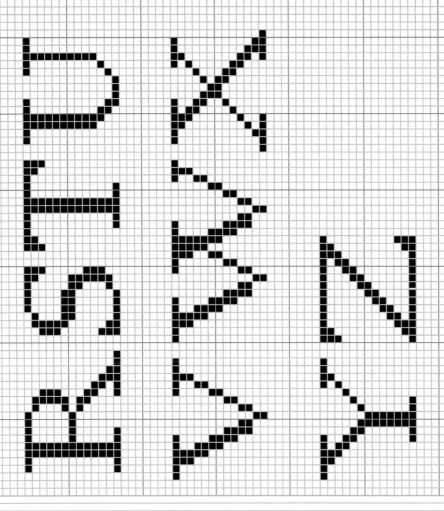

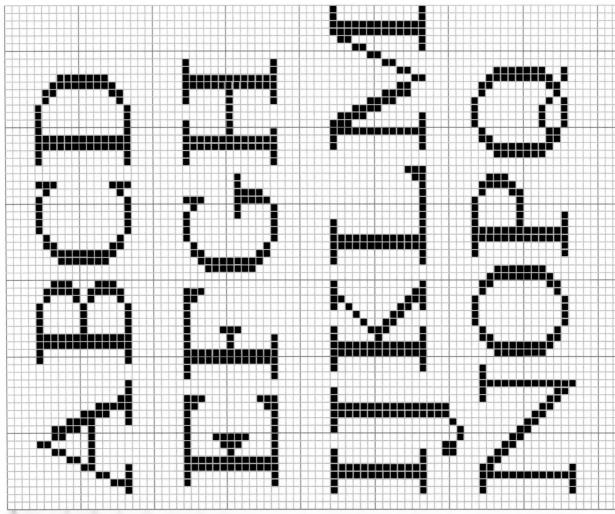

HEART SACHET

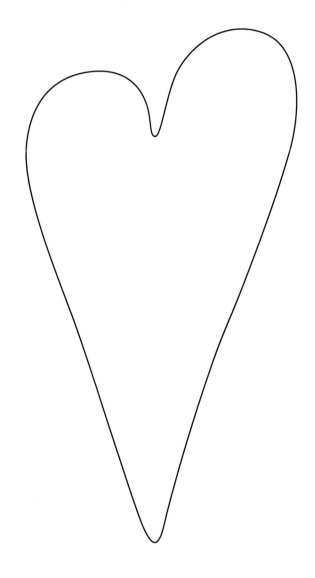